For Nelson Molina, who sees beauty everywhere.
—AL


To my family, the best ones.
—OV

Published by Sourcebooks eXplore, an imprint of Sourcebooks Kids
P.O. Box 4410, Naperville, Illinois 60567-4410
(630) 961-3900
sourcebookskids.com
Cataloging-in-Publication Data is on file with the Library of Congress.
Source of Production: Wing King Tong Paper Products Co. Ltd., Shenzhen, Guangdong Province, China
Date of Production: March 2024
Run Number: 5037509
Printed and bound in China.
WKT 10 9 8 7 6 5 4 3 2 1

# Gifts *from the* Garbage Truck

## A TRUE STORY ABOUT THE THINGS WE (DON'T) THROW AWAY

Words by
**Andrew Larsen**

Foreword by
**Nelson Molina**

Pictures by
**Oriol Vidal**

sourcebooks eXplore

I was born and raised in New York City in East Harlem, in a neighborhood called El Barrio (the Neighborhood) in Spanish. Many of my neighbors in the community, like my parents, were originally from Puerto Rico. *Gifts from the Garbage Truck* is the story of how I created Treasures in the Trash, an amazing museum of forty-five thousand items that I found in the garbage of El Barrio. I cleaned, repaired, and arranged the objects over my thirty-four years as a New York City sanitation worker. There's nothing in the world quite like it.

Growing up, we didn't have a lot. When I was a child, my mother taught me not to waste anything we could use again and to repair what could be saved. We didn't look at things and say, "This is worthless." Instead, we looked for the value in everything. My mother always kept boxes of outgrown clothes that she would share with others on our family Lotería (bingo) nights. I once watched her fix a broken toaster using a butter knife instead of a screwdriver because we didn't have any tools. Following her lead, when I was about ten years old, I started looking through old toys people had thrown out. I would bring some back to my five brothers and sisters. I could see how much joy it brought them, and that brought me joy too.

Once I became a sanitation worker, I continued doing what I'd done since childhood: taking things out of the trash to give them another life. This was the perfect job for me! I hope you also find something you love and are good at, then follow that into a job you love when you grow up.

Today, all kinds of people come to see my collection of objects I saved from the garbage. I love when a visitor sees something that sparks a memory of their life in New York. With joy on our faces, we talk about it and become friends. I also try to arrange things beautifully so that visitors will pause and think about the "trash" in their lives. I hope they leave considering how they might reuse, recycle, or upcycle more, finding beauty in the things they used to think of as garbage.

As you grow up, start to look for the value in everything! Before you say it's worthless, try to give it a new life. And remember, there is beauty in the world around you, and it's worth sharing.

Nelson Molina

Nelson Molina collected things.

He collected all kinds of things.

Like the scraps of wood he found
on his way to school.

Nelson's mom showed him how to use scraps of wood to make birdhouses.

"If someone can use it, don't throw it away," she liked to say.

She was an expert at reusing and recycling.

Nelson's dad was a merchant marine.

He traveled the world on a great big ship and sent letters home to Nelson.

Nelson collected every stamp from every letter.

He displayed some stamps by color.

He displayed some stamps by theme, like birds and boats.

The displays told stories about the faraway places his dad had been

Nelson was checking on his birdhouses when he
something in a trash can.

toy garbage truck that was missing a wheel.

uld anyone *throw this away?* Nelson wondered. *I know
e who would love it.*

Nelson cleaned the truck when he got home.

He painted it white, just like a New York City garbage truck.

Then he found a big button to replace the missing wheel.

It looked as good as new.

Nelson gave it to his little brother.

"I love it!" said his brother, eyes wide with wonder.

It was snowy in New York City in the weeks before Christmas.

People were throwing away old toys to make room for new ones.

Nelson had a better idea.

On Christmas morning, Nelson had a gift for each of his siblings.

Each gift had been found and fixed.

Each had a story.

Each was special in its own way.

When Nelson grew up, he didn't travel the world on a great big ship.

He became a trash collector.

His official title was New York City Sanitation Worker.

He rode around in a great big garbage truck, working on the streets where he used to play.

Everything he loved was right there, in his own neighborhood.

Being a trash collector was hard work.

There were tons of trash to collect each day.

Nelson worked in the heat, the cold, the rain, and the snow.

He filled up his garbage truck and then drove it to the dump.

At the dump, everything was put into containers and shipped out of town.

Some of it was burned and turned into electricity.

Some of it was buried deep underground.

And some of it was recycled.

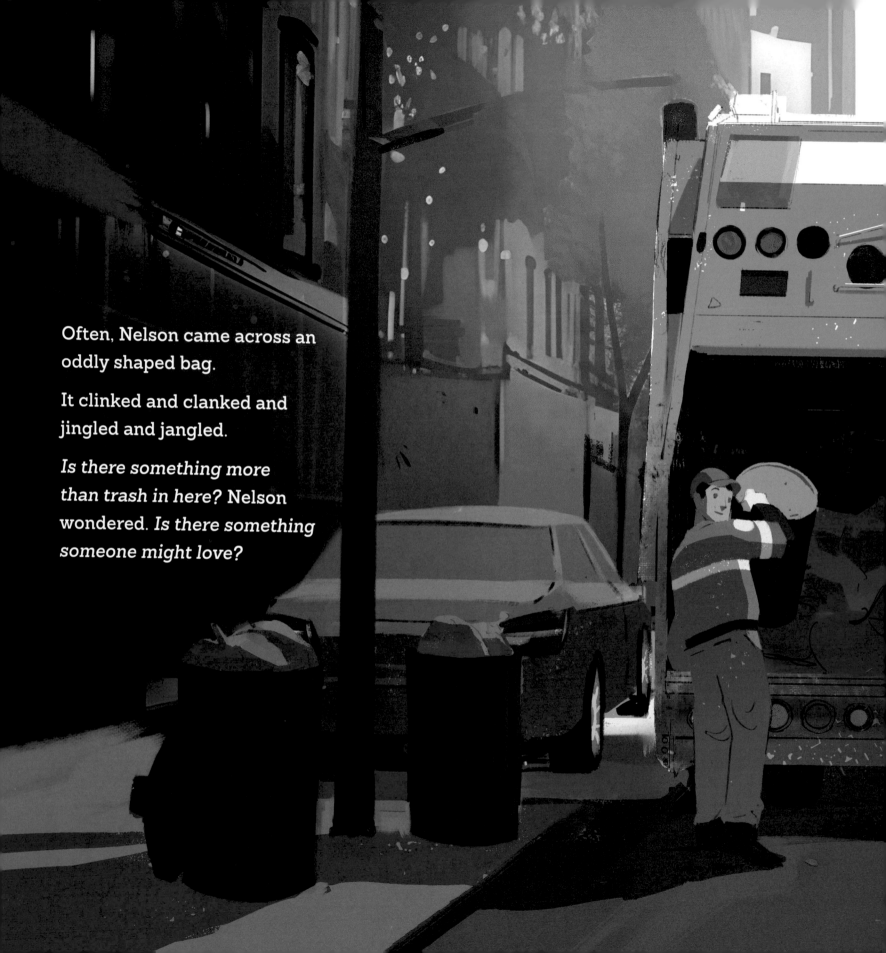

Often, Nelson came across an oddly shaped bag.

It clinked and clanked and jingled and jangled.

*Is there something more than trash in here?* Nelson wondered. *Is there something someone might love?*

"I knew it!" he exclaimed, tearing the bag open. "A gift from the garbage."

Nelson didn't throw these gifts into the back of the truck with everything else.

He had a better idea.

Nelson brought the objects he found back to the sanitation garage.

He displayed them in the locker room so everyone at work could see them.

There were toys and teapots.

Yo-yos and photos.

There were knick-knacks and thingamajigs and whatchamacallits.

People throw away the most extraordinary things.

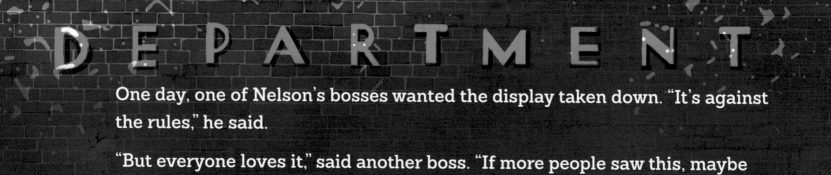

DEPARTMENT

One day, one of Nelson's bosses wanted the display taken down. "It's against the rules," he said.

"But everyone loves it," said another boss. "If more people saw this, maybe they'd think twice about the things they throw away."

The display stayed.

Sometimes an object Nelson found was broken or needed extra care.

He was happy to repair it.

He was even happier it wasn't going to the dump.

Each object was special in its own way, and Nelson found a place for them all.

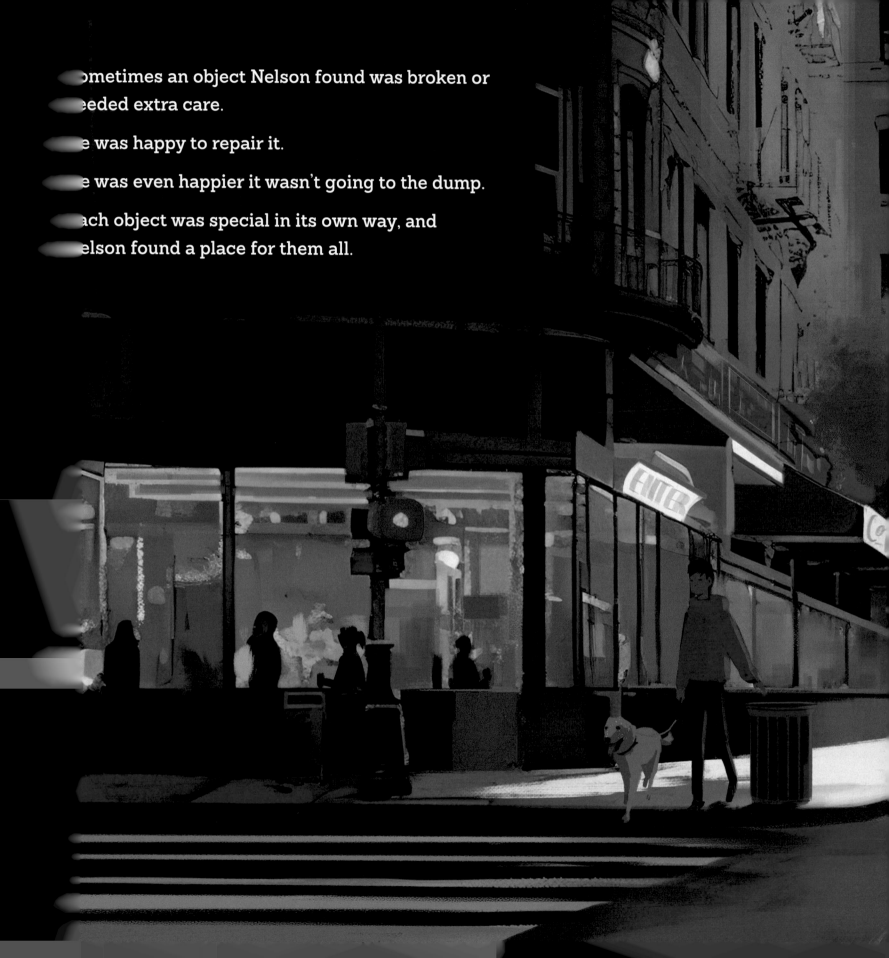

Piece by piece, year after year, Nelson's collection grew.

It grew from the locker room into the offices and stairwells.

It grew into the main garage.

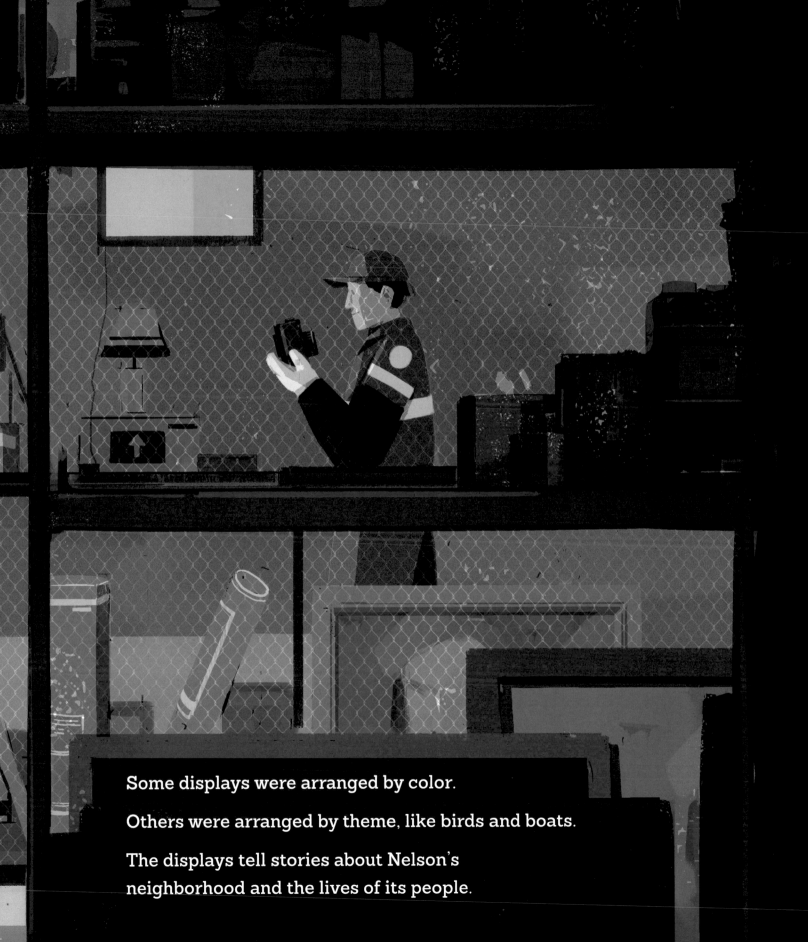

Some displays were arranged by color.

Others were arranged by theme, like birds and boats.

The displays tell stories about Nelson's neighborhood and the lives of its people.

Nelson's extraordinary collection has grown up to become a museum.

People from all around the world come to see it.

It's not far from the Metropolitan Museum of Art.

It's an invitation to think differently about the things we throw away.

It's Nelson Molina's gift to us all.

# THE 4 RS: REDUCE, REUSE, RECYCLE, AND RETHINK

There are many ways each of us can slow waste production and help our planet.

**Reduce**: Use only what you need, and don't be wasteful.

**Reuse**: Keep using something instead of throwing it away. You can use that object for the same purpose or a new purpose.

**Recycle**: Learn what can be separated from the rest of your waste, so it can be collected, processed, and turned into new products.

**Rethink**: Be mindful of how your daily choices impact our planet.

Nelson Molina is a rethinker and a reuser. He knows there is value in many things we throw away. He assembled a collection of objects he found in others' trash, and that collection became a museum.

## UPCYCLING

*Upcycling* is a particular way of *reusing*. Instead of throwing something away, use your imagination to transform that object into something even more valuable. Upcycling is often creative and crafty. It might take time and effort, but it's worth it.

## DON'T THROW THAT AWAY!

- Use an old map as gift wrap.

- Tie-dye a tired T-shirt.

- Paint a piece of beat-up furniture.

- Turn a rain boot into a flowerpot.

- Fix a broken toy.

- Cut the legs off a pair of long pants to turn them into a pair of shorts.

- Make a bird feeder out of an old soda bottle.

- Use cutlery to make a wind chime.

- Turn a tin can into a lantern.

- Use a clean jam jar as a pencil holder.

- Take a stamp from an envelope and start your own stamp collection.

# TREASURES IN THE TRASH

New York City Garbage Truck

Nelson and Nelson Jr.

The Museum

Nelson

More Treasures!